Speed Training
for Teen Athletes
Exercises to Take Your Game to the Next Level

by Shane Frederick

Consultant:
Thomas Inkrott
Head Strength and Conditioning Coach
Minnesota State University, Mankato

CAPSTONE PRESS
a capstone imprint

Sports Illustrated Kids Sports Training Zone is published by Capstone Press,
1710 Roe Crest Drive, North Mankato, Minnesota 56003.
www.capstonepress.com

Books published by Capstone Press are manufactured with paper
containing at least 10 percent post-consumer waste.

Library of Congress Cataloging-in-Publication Data
Frederick, Shane.
  Speed training for teen athletes : exercises to take your game to the next level / by Shane Frederick.
    p. cm.—(Sports illustrated kids. sports training zone.)
  Includes bibliographical references and index.
  ISBN 978-1-4296-7678-6 (library binding)
  ISBN 978-1-4296-7999-2 (paperback)
  1. Teenage athletes—Training of—Juvenile literature. 2. Speed—Juvenile literature.
  I. Title. II. Series.
  GV711.5.F733 2012
  613.711—dc23   2011033558

Editorial Credits
Anthony Wacholtz, editor; Heidi Thompson, designer; Eric Gohl, media researcher;
    Marcy Morin, scheduler; Laura Manthe, production specialist

Photo Credits
TJ Thoraldson Digital Photography, all interior training photos

iStockphoto: Prokhorov, design element (backgrounds); Shutterstock: Jaimie Duplass, 44,
Vita Khorzhevska, 35; Sports Illustrated: Al Tielemans, 16, 34, Bill Frakes, cover (bottom
left), 5, Bob Martin, 45, Chuck Solomon, cover (bottom middle right), 17, David E.
Klutho, cover (bottom middle), back cover, 27, John Biever, cover (top, bottom middle left,
bottom right), John W. McDonough, 6, Robert Beck, 26, Simon Bruty, 7

Printed in the United States of America in North Mankato, Minnesota.
102011   006405CGS12

TABLE of CONTENTS

WHAT IS
Speed
Training?

It's often said in sports that if you're faster than your opponent, you have an advantage. But speed doesn't only mean running fast. It includes your overall quickness—from running forward and backward to starting, stopping, and changing directions. Speed is demonstrated in your ability to **accelerate** and in your explosive power when you jump, spike, and swing.

This book will show you ways to improve your overall athletic speed, no matter what you're training for. Even if you're not practicing for a specific sport, the exercises should be fun. They are also a good way to get some of the regular exercise you need each day.

Are You Ready?

Before you begin training, ask yourself the following questions: Is your body ready for speed training? What are you training for? What muscles do you need to use and how will you be using them? Are you strong enough? Are you in shape? If you are new to exercising and training, make sure you start slowly. Don't do too much too soon!

Before you begin any of these exercises, it's important to warm up. Get your blood pumping and your heart beating a little harder. Do a set of jumping jacks and go for a light run or jog in place. Do this for about 10 minutes. Now you're ready for your workout.

EXERCISES ARE OFTEN DONE IN SETS, WITH A NUMBER OF **REPETITIONS**, OR REPS, IN EACH SET. BE SURE TO PACE YOURSELF BY RESTING FOR ONE OR TWO MINUTES BETWEEN EACH SET.

While you are doing your speed training, be sure to concentrate on technique and form. Doing the exercise correctly is more important than how hard or how fast you do it. Your goal is to run faster, jump higher, and swing harder. But you also want to do those things efficiently, without wasting energy. Remember: Quality is more important than quantity.

U.S. OLYMPIC RUNNER ANGELO TAYLOR

When your drills are done, spend another 10 minutes or so cooling down. Jog or walk. Then stretch your muscles. Stretching will help prevent injuries.

FACT: Be sure to include a proper warm-up and cool down fo your workout.
- Warm-up: 10–15 minutes
- Speed train: 20–30 minutes
- Cool-down: 10–15 minutes

ACCELERATE—TO MOVE FASTER OVER TIME
REPETITIONS—THE NUMBER OF TIMES AN EXERCISE IS DONE

Foot Speed, Quickness, and Agility

Professional basketball players are known for their quickness. They need fast feet to go a short distance, often racing an opposing player to a spot on the floor. The winner of that race might give himself an open jump shot or a chance to drive to the basket for a dunk. A point guard might draw another defender to her, allowing her to make an assist.

For a player on defense, quicker feet can mean stopping a scoring opportunity. It might be the difference between forcing a turnover and committing a costly foul. Many players have had trouble defending Chicago Bulls superstar guard Derrick Rose. He has made defenders look silly with his crossover dribble. The move gets his opponent leaning or stepping one way. Then Rose quickly changes direction, while the defender gets his legs tangled or even falls to the floor.

NBA GUARD
DERRICK ROSE

Soccer players also need quick feet when dribbling the ball and defending. Tennis and badminton players use foot speed and **agility** as well. They need to quickly cover the court and set themselves for powerful return shots. Football and lacrosse players rely on agility to constantly stop, start, and change directions.

SOCCER STAR
ABBY WAMBACH

AGILITY—THE ABILITY TO MOVE QUICKLY AN

JUMP ROPE

20–30 MINUTES

There are several exercises you can do with a jump rope to quicken your feet. Boxers often jump rope in order to stay light on their feet and improve their balance. The exercise can benefit soccer, basketball, and lacrosse players who are constantly moving their feet and changing direction. Jumping rope is also a great way to get your heart pumping!

WHAT YOU'LL NEED

• jump rope

EXERCISE 1: Two-leg jump: Jump with both feet.

Exercise Daily

According to the Centers for Disease Control, teens should get one hour or more of physical activity each day. That includes:
- Aerobic activity (walking, running, playing a sport) at least three days a week
- Muscle strengthening (gymnastics, pushups) at least three days a week
- Bone strengthening (jumping rope, running) at least three days a week

EXERCISE 2: One-leg jump: Jump with one foot lifted behind you.

EXERCISE 3: High knees: Run in place, bringing your knees up as high as possible.

EXERCISE 4:
Crossover: After three or four jumps with two feet, cross your arms and jump through the loop. Then uncross your arms and jump two or three times before crossing your arms again.

TIP:
Try going 20 seconds at a time with one minute of rest between jumping.

SHUTTLE RUN
20–30 MINUTES

This drill is similar to a race you might have run in your school gym class. It involves both straight-ahead speed—called linear speed—and changing directions quickly. This will help improve starts, stops, and cuts.

1 Start at the middle cone.

WHAT YOU'LL NEED

- place with enough space to sprint at least 20 yards
- three cones or other markers set up 5 yards apart

VARIATION

IF YOU'RE A FOOTBALL PLAYER, YOU MIGHT WANT TO START IN A THREE-POINT STANCE AS YOU WOULD WHILE PLAYING A GAME.

2. Dash five yards to one cone. Reach down and touch the marker.

3. Reverse direction and sprint 10 yards to the far cone. Reach down and touch the marker.

4. Reverse direction and sprint hard 10 yards past the marker. Rest for two to four minutes. Repeat up to 10 times.

TIP:

Use a stopwatch to see how long it takes to do each run. Add up your totals in one training session and record your average time. See if you can lower your average time throughout your training.

SPEED LADDER

20–30 MINUTES

Like a jump rope, a speed ladder allows you to perform several drills to improve your foot speed and agility. But this is not a ladder you climb. Lay the ladder down on a flat surface to perform these quickness drills.

WHAT YOU'LL NEED

- speed ladder (10, 20, or 30 feet)

For all of the ladder exercises, make sure you:
1. Keep your head and eyes up, looking at the end of the course. Don't look at your feet.
2. Pump your arms and hands throughout the drill.
4. Do the drills in intervals, resting between drills.

EXERCISE 1: One foot per box. Run the length of the ladder with one step in each box.

TIP:

You can also use tape or pavement chalk to sketch out a ladder on the sidewalk. But remember to concentrate on form and lift your feet above the "rungs."

EXERCISE 2: Two feet per box. Run the length of the ladder with two steps in each box.

BOTH EXERCISES:

Sprint up to five more yards after stepping out of the last box.

VARIATION

To increase intensity and build power in your legs, do the one- and two-foot drills with high knees. With each step, lift your opposite knee up to your chest.

ICKEY SHUFFLE

In the late 1980s, Cincinnati Bengals running back Ickey Woods entertained crowds with a touchdown celebration called the Ickey Shuffle. He rocked from side to side with quick steps and a little flair. Today athletes from many sports imitate Woods' dance on a speed ladder to improve their footwork.

WHAT YOU'LL NEED

- speed ladder

1. Start by standing outside the ladder to the right of a box.

2. Step sideways into the box, first with your left foot, and then your right foot.

3. With your left foot, step outside the ladder to the left of the next box. Follow with your right foot.

4. Step into the second box with your right foot. Follow with your left foot.

5. With your right foot, step outside the ladder to the right of the second box. Repeat these steps for each box of the ladder.

VARIATION

You can add some difficulty to the exercise by adding one of these variations:

1. Rotate a tennis ball around your waist.
2. Have a partner throw a tennis ball to you, then play catch at a slow pace.

Running Faster, Jumping Higher

With a 2010 football game tied 31-31 and only 14 seconds to go in the game, the New York Giants were forced to punt to the Philadelphia Eagles. Both teams expected the game to go into overtime. The Eagles' punt returner DeSean Jackson dropped the ball when it got to him. He picked up the ball and went backward four yards as the Giants players closed in on him.

But then Jackson sprinted forward, accelerating to full speed and outrunning everyone to the end zone. He crossed the goal line as time expired, and his touchdown won the game for the Eagles.

Jackson is one of the fastest players in the National Football League (NFL). But nearly everyone at that level can run a 40-yard dash in less than five seconds. So how do speedy kick returners and wide receivers maintain their explosive edge? By training their legs for speed.

NFL WIDE RECEIVER
DeSean Jackson

Football players aren't alone in this kind of training. Sprinters on track teams need straight-ahead speed, as do hockey and lacrosse players. Baseball and softball players need speed on the base paths and the outfield. Speed work is also important for athletes who jump, such as gymnasts and volleyball players.

SPRINT INTERVALS

20–30 MINUTES

Improving your straight-ahead speed will help you in many sports. The simplest exercise you can do is run sprints. *Interval* training combines running as fast as you can with rest and recovery time. Sprint intervals will not only make you faster over time but will also improve your endurance. That way you'll be effective at the beginning and end of the event.

WHAT YOU'LL NEED

- place with enough space to sprint for 30 seconds, such as a track or athletic field

INTERVAL—THE SPACE OR TIME BETWEEN TWO POINTS

1. After a proper warm-up, sprint for 30 seconds at 60 percent intensity. Walk for two minutes.

2. Sprint for 30 seconds at 80 percent intensity. Walk for two minutes.

3. Sprint for 30 seconds at your top speed (100 percent intensity).

4. Walk for two to four minutes. You should be able to breathe normally. Repeat steps 3 and 4 up to eight times.

VARIATION

START SMALL AND BUILD. WHEN THE EXERCISE STARTS TO GET EASIER FOR YOU, TRY SPRINTING IN AN AREA WITH A SLIGHT INCLINE AND RUN UPHILL.

The Importance of Breathing

You might not have to remember to breathe as you go about your day. But when you exercise it helps to concentrate on breathing. Oxygen is fuel for your muscles—make sure they're getting the air they need. Breathe in and out throughout your drills.

LATERAL JUMPS

3 SETS OF 8–10 REPS

Your muscles are made up of muscle fibers. The fibers are long, threadlike cells that are bundled together and work to move your body. The fibers twitch to make your muscles contract. But they don't twitch at the same rate. There are fast- and slow-twitch fibers. To improve speed and explosive power, you need to train the fast-twitch fibers. Plyometric jumping does that.

WHAT YOU'LL NEED

- exercise box or shoebox

1. Stand on one side of the box with your feet together.

TIP:
If you're not comfortable jumping over an object, you can jump over a line on a gym floor. You can also use tape or chalk to make a line. But make sure to jump high in the air.

2. Jump sideways as high as you can across the box. You should land with your feet on the ground next to the box.

3. Immediately jump back to the other side of the box. That is one rep.

How Do Plyos Work?

Many of the drills in this book are plyometric exercises. Plyometrics—sometimes called plyos— are high-intensity workouts that focus on explosive muscle movements. Many of the exercises feature hops, leaps, jumps, and bursts that will improve your overall athletic performance, including speed.

To better understand plyometrics, think of your muscles and tendons as rubber bands. When you pull back a rubber band, energy is stored in the stretched-out band. When you let go, it uses the energy to snap back into shape. Plyometrics train your muscles to work in that same explosive fashion.

BOUNDS

3 SETS AT 25–30 YARDS – – – – – – – – – –

The explosive power that helps you run is used in many sports. The power comes from the muscles and tendons in your legs. Bounds focus on that power by exaggerating your running motions. With each step, spring forward with high knees and oversized strides.

WHAT YOU'LL NEED

- 30 yards of open space, such as a track or athletic field

1. Start by pushing off your right foot.

2. Bring your left leg forward with your knee bent and your thigh parallel to the ground.

TIP:
Wear comfortable, proper-fitting athletic shoes that help absorb some of the shock from the bounds.

3. When you land, spring to your next step as quickly as possible. Push off your left foot and bring your right leg forward.

4. Bound for 25 to 30 yards.

Staying Hydrated

When you exercise you lose fluids that your body needs. Replace the liquid by drinking water or a sports drink before, during, and after your workout. Don't wait until you're thirsty, or you may become dehydrated.

SQUAT JUMPS

3 SETS OF 10 REPS

Speed isn't just about going fast. There are only a few sports in which athletes get up to full speed. That's why it's important to focus on explosive speed and the ability to get to a spot as quickly as possible. Whether you play in sneakers, cleats, or skates, squat jumps will help you accelerate faster.

1. Stand with your feet shoulder-width apart.

2. Squat down as if you're sitting in a chair. Keep your thighs parallel to the floor.

3. Jump straight up as high as possible.

4. When you land, return to the squat and jump again.

TIP:
Don't stop between jumps. Your feet should be on the floor for as little time as possible as you do plyometric exercises.

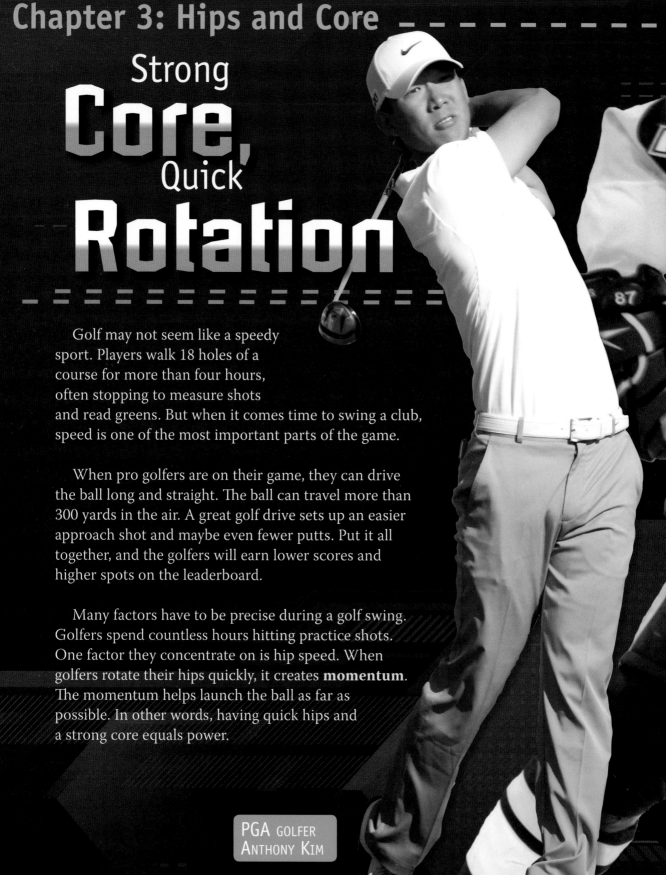

Strong Core, Quick Rotation

Golf may not seem like a speedy sport. Players walk 18 holes of a course for more than four hours, often stopping to measure shots and read greens. But when it comes time to swing a club, speed is one of the most important parts of the game.

When pro golfers are on their game, they can drive the ball long and straight. The ball can travel more than 300 yards in the air. A great golf drive sets up an easier approach shot and maybe even fewer putts. Put it all together, and the golfers will earn lower scores and higher spots on the leaderboard.

Many factors have to be precise during a golf swing. Golfers spend countless hours hitting practice shots. One factor they concentrate on is hip speed. When golfers rotate their hips quickly, it creates **momentum**. The momentum helps launch the ball as far as possible. In other words, having quick hips and a strong core equals power.

PGA GOLFER
ANTHONY KIM

Baseball and softball hitters also work on their hip rotation to help their bat speed. Hockey players need strong hips for quick starts and stops and strong cores for balance when the games become physical. Football kickers and soccer strikers also need strong hips for booting the ball.

NHL CENTER
SIDNEY CROSBY

MOMENTUM—THE STRENGTH OR FORCE SOMETHING HAS WHEN IT IS MOVING

LUNGES

3 SETS OF 8–10 REPS

Stretching and strengthening your hip flexors is important to improve performance in almost every sport. Hip flexors are groups of muscles around the pelvic area that allow you to lift your legs and bring your knees up toward your waist. Keeping them stretched and limber helps any athlete who has to run for a sport. It's also good for hockey players' skating stride.

WHAT YOU'LL NEED

• set of dumbbells, three to five pounds each (optional)

1. Stand with your legs spread slightly.

2. Lunge forward with one leg. Make sure your knee doesn't stick out farther than your toe. Bend your knees until your back knee almost touches the floor. Keep your back straight.

3. Stand up again, bringing your feet back to starting position.

4. Repeat steps two through four with the other leg. That is one rep.

VARIATION

Hold dumbbells in your hands and do the lunges as you walk. Carrying the extra weight while walking will help build strength in your hips and upper body.

HIP CROSSOVER

3 SETS OF 10–12 REPS

Hip crossovers can help your hips and lower body work independently of your upper body. A softball player steps forward while twisting her torso on her swing. A running back keeps his shoulders square while his hips swivel to avoid tackles. Both movements require quick hips, and hip crossovers are the key.

WHAT YOU'LL NEED

• floor mat (optional)

1. Lie on your back with arms spread wide and both shoulders on the ground. Keep your palms on the ground. Bend your knees, lift your toes, and keep your heels on the ground.

2. Keeping your back straight, rotate your hips to the left. Let your knees fall to the ground. Make sure your shoulders are touching the ground.

3. Repeat step 2, this time rotating your hips to the right. Rotating your hips each way once is one rep.

VARIATIONS

VARIATION 1: LIFT YOUR FEET OFF THE GROUND, KEEPING YOUR KNEES BENT AT 90 DEGREES BEFORE ROTATING.

VARIATION 2: LIFT YOUR LEGS STRAIGHT IN THE AIR BEFORE ROTATING.

WOOD CHOPS

3 SETS OF 6–8 REPS

The wood chop is an exercise that strengthens the hips, as well as core muscles such as **abdominals** and **obliques**. But it also mimics explosive speed movements in many sports. It's the same movement a volleyball player uses to smash an overhead serve for an ace. Time to chop some wood. But instead of an ax, you'll use a medicine ball.

WHAT YOU'LL NEED

- medicine ball

1. Stand up straight with your feet shoulder-width apart. Hold the medicine ball in front of you with both hands.

2. Lift the medicine ball up over one shoulder.

3. Swing your arms down across your body. Rotate your torso so that the ball ends up at your opposite hip.

4. Bring the ball back up over your shoulder again.

5. After one set, repeat steps 2 through 4, but swing the medicine ball across your body in the opposite direction.

TIP:
Start with a five-pound medicine ball. Once you master the exercise, use a slightly heavier ball.

ABDOMINALS—THE MUSCLES BELOW THE CHEST IN THE STOMACH AREA; ALSO CALLED ABS

OBLIQUES—THE MUSCLES ON THE SIDES OF THE TRUNK, ABOVE THE HIPS AND NEAR THE RIB CAGE

Throw
Faster,
Move Quicker

In 2010 Cincinnati Reds pitcher Aroldis Chapman did something no other pitcher done before. He threw a scorching pitch the San Diego Padres' Tony Gwynn Jr. zoomed by in the blink of an eye. ball traveled the 60 feet, 6 inches Chapman's hand to the catcher record 105 miles per hour. Just impressive, Chapman threw astballs that night that went er than 100 mph.

he following spring a radar gun at cinnati's Great American Ballpark ked a Chapman pitch at 106 mph. hough that speed wasn't official, few bted that Chapman could throw that hard.

What does it take to throw a baseball fast? You must e proper form and use muscles throughout your body, uding your legs. But you also need excellent arm speed et the ball moving. A batter trying to hit that fireball relies on arm and hand speed to get his bat on the before it ends up in the catcher's mitt.

MLB PITCHER
AROLDIS CHAPMAN

Just as you would train your legs to get quicker, you can train your upper body to get faster. Other athletes who rely on arm speed include quarterbacks and linemen, boxers, martial artists, hockey players, and swimmers.

MEDICINE BALL CHEST PASS

3 SETS OF 10–20 REPS

WHAT YOU'LL NEED

- medicine ball

Many sports require athletes to use their hands. Whether they're football linemen who are blocking or people who practice **martial arts**, athletes need explosive speed from their hands. This plyometric exercise is a good way to improve that quickness and power.

1. Stand four to five feet away from a partner. Stand with your feet shoulder-width apart and with your knees slightly bent.

2. Bring the ball to your chest and fire the ball to your partner.

3. The receiver should catch the ball and allow it to come all the way to his or her chest and, as quickly as possible, send it back. Try not to pause between passes (but be careful).

VARIATION

IF YOU DON'T HAVE A PARTNER TO PASS THE BALL TO, TRY USING THE WALL INSTEAD. YOU CAN ALSO TRY THE EXERCISE WHILE YOU'RE SEATED.

TIP:

When you do exercises with medicine balls, start with lighter weights until you are ready for heavier balls.

MARTIAL ARTS—FIGHTING AND SELF DEFENSE SPORTS, INCLUDING KARATE, JUDO, AND TAE KWAN DO

BICEP CURLS

3 SETS OF 8–10 REPS

There are dozens of exercises you can do with elastic resistance bands or any kind of rubber cord. Bicep curls are a great way to start. Not only will this exercise build strength in your arms, but it will also improve flexibility in your shoulders and elbows. The increased strength and flexibility will enhance your speed in many sports.

WHAT YOU'LL NEED

• resistance band

1. Stand up straight with your feet shoulder-width apart. Place the middle of the resistance band under the arches of your feet. Hold the handles (ends) in each hand. Start with your arms hanging down.

2. Starting with your right arm, slowly do a curl as you would with a dumbbell. Bend your elbows and bring your hand up to your chest.

TIP:

Resistance bands come in various degrees of resistance. Start small and increase the difficulty as you get stronger.

3. Repeat step 2 with your left arm. Alternate curls between your left and right arms. A curl with each arm is one rep.

Imitate Your Sport!

Some of the best training involves exercises that imitate the movements you use while playing sports. The movements can include sprinting, cutting, throwing, or swinging. These drills improve speed and quickness, but they also train your muscles to make the movements naturally. This process is called muscle memory, and it comes in handy when you use those actions in competition.

You can use a resistance band for many muscle memory exercises. Secure one end of a band to a stable object, such as a fence post. Grip the other end and make throwing, punching, or swinging motions for the sport you're training for. Don't forget to concentrate on proper technique as you mimic those movements.

PUSH-UPS

20–30 REPS

Building up your total upper-body strength is a great way to increase speed for throwing balls or swinging bats, sticks, or rackets. One of the simplest ways to do that is with the reliable push-up. This old-fashioned exercise works your arms, shoulders, and chest.

WHAT YOU'LL NEED

- space to lie down

1. Lie face down on the floor with your feet slightly apart. Place your hands flat on the floor slightly under and slightly wider than your shoulders.

2. Keeping your back straight, push yourself up until your arms are straight.

3. Slowly lower yourself back down, stopping just a couple of inches from the floor.

4. Push yourself back up again. Count how many you can do before needing a break. Your endurance should improve over time. After some rest and recovery time, try again.

VARIATIONS

You can make your push-ups a plyometric exercise by adding a clap. When you push up, quickly clap your hands together and get them back to the floor before your body hits the floor. You can also try doing a push-up with your knees on the ground instead of your toes.

BEAR CRAWLS

20–30 MINUTES

You can get your trusty speed ladder out again for more upper-body drills. This time you'll get down on all fours and bear crawl on your hands and feet. Crawl the length of the ladder to work your hands, arms, and upper body.

WHAT YOU'LL NEED

• speed ladder

For both of the ladder exercises, make sure you:

1. Keep your head and eyes up, looking at the end of the course.

2. Do the drills in intervals.

EXERCISE 1: One hand per box. Bear crawl the length of the ladder, placing one hand in each box. Alternate left and right hands.

EXERCISE 2: Two hands per box.
Bear crawl the length of the ladder,
placing two hands in each box.

VARIATION

You can do a hand version of the Ickey Shuffle. Follow the same left-right pattern found on pages 14 and 15.

Repair and Rebuild

Just as each of the exercises has breaks built in for a breather, it's equally important to have full days devoted to rest and recovery. Training hard every single day of the week can be bad for you. It may cause you to feel tired and weak or make you prone to injuries. Your body needs rest and recovery time to repair and rebuild sore muscles and to strengthen the areas you've worked hard to train.

Elite athletes might use their rest days to relax their muscles in a hot tub or with a massage. If you don't have those opportunities, you shouldn't do "nothing" on your rest day. Go for a walk or a light bike ride. Take some time to stretch out your muscles. Whatever you do, stay active—just don't overdo it!

Listen to Your Body

Your body will let you know when something is wrong. Be sure to listen to it. Any pain in your knees, ankles, elbows, or wrists is a sign you should stop what you're doing. If the pain doesn't go away, you should see a doctor or an athletic trainer.

Your muscles might get sore from your speed exercises, especially when you first start. That is normal. But other signs of injury can include tenderness, swelling, weakness, numbness, and difficulty moving a certain part of your body. Be on the lookout for those symptoms. You don't want to continue your training if you have a muscle pull or a joint injury.

TENNIS STAR
SERENA WILLIAMS

Speed in sports doesn't just come naturally. It takes dedication and determination to get the legs of Chris Johnson or Serena Williams or the feet of Kobe Bryant or Landon Donovan. You can't get the arms of Misty May-Treanor or Michael Phelps or the hands of Joe Mauer or Manny Pacquiao overnight. So work hard, but have fun too!

Glossary

abdominals—the muscles below the chest in the stomach area; also called abs

accelerate—to move faster over time

agility—the ability to move quickly and easily

fiber—a thin thread used to form tissues in the body

form—a manner or style of performing

hydrate—to achieve a healthy balance of fluids in the body

intensity—the amount of strength something has

interval—the space or time between two points

linear—relating to a straight line

martial arts—fighting and self-defense sports

medicine ball—weighted ball used for training and exercise; also called an exercise ball

momentum—the strength or force something has when it is moving

muscle memory—when your muscles are trained to move in a specific way for something

obliques—side abdominal muscles that help you bend and rotate your torso

repetitions—the number of times an exercise is done in a set; also called reps

rotate—to move or turn in a circle or back and forth in an arc

technique—way or method of doing something that requires skill

Read More

Mason, Paul. *Improving Speed*. Training for Sports. New York: PowerKids Press, 2011.

Payment, Simone. *What Happens to Your Body When You Run*. The How and Why of Exercise. New York: Rosen Central, 2010.

Shaffer, Alyssa. *Feeling Great: A Girl's Guide to Fitness, Friends & Fun*. Middleton, Wis.: American Girl Publishing, 2010.

St. Germain, Wendy. *Talking about Exercise*. Healthy Living. New York: Gareth Stevens Pub., 2010.

Internet Sites

FactHound offers a safe, fun way to find Internet sites related to this book. All of the sites on FactHound have been researched by our staff.

Here's all you do:

Visit *www.facthound.com*

Type in this code: 9781429676786

Index